★ *Asian American Women in Science* ★

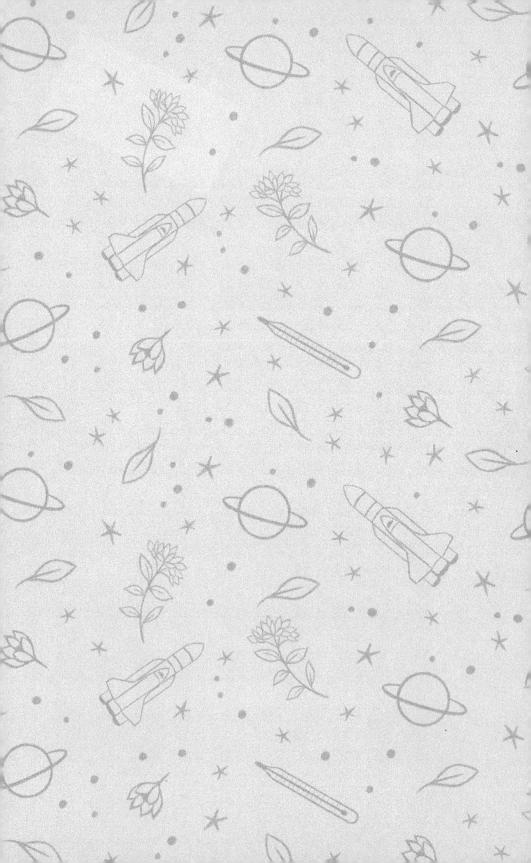

Asian American Women IN SCIENCE

AN ASIAN AMERICAN HISTORY BOOK FOR KIDS

Tina Cho

Illustrations by María Díaz Perera

ROCKRIDGE
PRESS

For general information on our other products and services or to obtain technical support, please contact our Customer Care Department within the United States at (866) 744-2665, or outside the United States at (510) 253-0500.

Rockridge Press publishes its books in a variety of electronic and print formats. Some content that appears in print may not be available in electronic books, and vice versa.

Series Designer: Will Mack
Interior and Cover Designer: Angela Navarra
Art Producer: Janice Ackerman
Editor: Erum Khan
Production Editor: Holland Baker
Production Manager: Riley Hoffman

Illustration © 2021 María Díaz Perera.
Author Photo Courtesy of Sarah B. Photography.

Paperback ISBN: 978-1-6387-8212-4
eBook ISBN: 978-1-63878-800-3
R0

This book is dedicated
to the Asian American
women scientists in this
book and future scientists
who are reading this book,
and to our Creator, who
created an amazing world
for us to explore.

Contents

Introduction

Throughout history, human progress has depended on advances in science. As scientists have made countless inventions and discoveries, they have improved the quality of our lives and our understanding of the universe around us. Asian American women have played a major role in this progress through their contributions to **STEM** (Science, Technology, Engineering, and Math) fields. They paved the way forward with new knowledge, improved education, and a deep curiosity about our world.

Because most people did not start immigrating from Asia to the United States until the late 19th century, the 15 Asian American researchers, doctors, mathematicians, and engineers profiled in this book are all from the 20th century and today. They are Japanese, Chinese, Indian, Korean, Iranian, Filipina, Hawaiian, and Taiwanese. They represent some (but by no means all) of the many time periods and scientific fields in which Asian American women have achieved greatness.

Dr. Kazue Togasaki was a brave and caring leader in trying times. Dr. Chien-Shiung Wu persisted even when her work went unrecognized. Dr. Isabella Aiona Abbott taught others her passion. And Dr. Margaret Chung made a way when things seemed impossible. By learning about their lives, struggles, and achievements, we can gain new perspectives on science and be inspired by their brilliance. Each woman overcame obstacles, and they encourage us to never give up on our dreams.

You'll learn all about these amazing trailblazers in the coming pages. Get ready to let these 15 biographies inspire YOU to scientific greatness!

Margaret
CHUNG
{ 1889–1959 }

Dr. Margaret Chung, the first Chinese American physician, broke barriers as a woman *and* as an Asian American. Not only was she a doctor, but she supported U.S. pilots during World War II and founded WAVES, a group that helped women join the navy. She was most famously known as "Mom Chung."

When Margaret was 10 years old, she knew she wanted to be a doctor, just like the one who made house calls on his bike to her family's California ranch. More specifically, Margaret wanted to be a medical **missionary** to China, the land where her parents were born. Like so many other Chinese people in that time, her parents had immigrated to the United States during the **California Gold Rush** and became Christians.

But it was a tough time for Chinese people to get jobs. In 1882, the United States passed the Chinese Exclusion Act, a law that banned immigrants from China coming to the United States to work. Employers wanted to give jobs to white people instead. To make money, Margaret's father became a vegetable peddler.

Being from a poor family did not stop Margaret from following her dream of becoming a doctor. Having no toys, she would take bananas and pretend to do surgery on them. As the oldest of 11 children, she cared for their mother when she was dying from **tuberculosis**. During these hard times, Margaret never gave up on her dream.

Margaret found a way to go to medical school. Selling newspaper subscriptions to the *Los Angeles Times* earned her a scholarship. She also worked in the school cafeteria, sold surgical equipment, and participated in speech contests to pay for her education. As the only woman in an all-male class, she dressed in men's clothing and called herself Mike to fit in. In 1916, Margaret completed the first step of her dream—graduating from medical school as the first Chinese American doctor in history!

"I'M AT MY BEST UNDER PRESSURE."

After graduating, she applied to be a medical missionary to China to help people and teach them about Christianity. But she was denied. The mission board wouldn't accept her because she wasn't white. So, she applied to medical **internships** in California hospitals.

Again, she was denied. But Margaret did not give up. She would find a way.

And she did. She got a job at a women's hospital in Chicago. After her internship, she moved back to California and worked as a plastic surgeon for famous Hollywood celebrities.

Margaret did not forget her calling to help Chinese people. In the early 1920s, she moved to San Francisco's Chinatown and opened a hospital. However, Chinese people did not want to go to her for medical care. Older people wanted doctors who used traditional Chinese medicine or herbs rather than Western medicine. Younger people wanted white doctors.

Eventually, though, Margaret proved herself with her skills, and business picked up. Non-Chinese patients visited, and the Chinese learned to trust her.

In 1931, Japan attacked China. China fought back with help from America. Margaret started supporting a group of seven pilots in the U.S. military. She often fed them dinner at her house and listened to their worries. They called her "Mom Chung" and became her "adopted" sons. Eventually, this little group of seven multiplied to over 1,000 men and women, even high-ranking officers, whom Margaret cared for.

During World War II, the government asked Margaret to recruit American pilots to fly fighter planes on behalf of China. After these men went off to war, she wrote them encouraging letters saying how proud she was of them. She plastered the notes they sent back to the walls of her office. Margaret mailed them care packages and Christmas gifts and never forgot their names. When her "sons" visited her, she gave them and their families homecooked meals.

Margaret didn't stop there. She wanted women to be allowed in the U.S. military, too. She introduced **legislation** to create WAVES—Women Accepted for Volunteer Emergency Services. The law would create a **reserve corps**, allowing women to join the navy. Margaret had influenced many celebrities through her plastic surgery practice, and they—along with her family of adopted children—helped her push for WAVES. President Franklin D. Roosevelt signed the legislation in 1942. But Margaret herself was never allowed to join the military because of her race and age.

Dr. Margaret Chung broke barriers as the first Chinese American doctor, the first woman doctor to practice in San Francisco's Chinatown, and a strong **advocate** for women to join the navy reserves. She refused to let **racism** or **sexism** stand in her way. Through lectures, radio programs, and writing, Margaret supported the United States and China during World War II—a war that they ultimately won. In 1945, Margaret received the "People's Medal" of the Chinese government.

Women today can join the military because of Dr. Margaret Chung. Asian American girls can grow up to become doctors because of her. Margaret was unstoppable until cancer took her life at the age of 69, but her legacy lives on. Margaret didn't let her humble beginnings or racial **prejudice** prevent her from achieving her dreams.

EXPLORE MORE! Learn about the history and culture of Chinese people in America by visiting the Museum of Chinese in America in New York. You can also learn a lot by visiting your city's local Chinatown.

DID YOU KNOW? Did you know that the actor John Wayne, Ronald Reagan, and pilot Amelia Earhart were some of the men and women among Margaret's "adopted children"?

Kazue
TOGASAKI
{ 1897–1992 }

Dr. Kazue Togasaki was one of the first Japanese American women doctors. She led the way in caring for Japanese Americans in **internment camps** during World War II. She also helped the struggling Asian American population after the war. She overcame great personal loss to become a leader and role model.

From her childhood in San Francisco, Kazue experienced racism. In elementary school, she, her brother, and another Japanese girl were forced to switch schools because some people didn't want white and Asian children learning in the same classroom.

Early in the morning on April 18, 1906, nine-year-old Kazue awoke to a violent earthquake in San Francisco. In less than a minute, much of the city was destroyed. Fires scorched everything. Buildings went up in flames. Debris covered the streets. Thousands of people were left homeless or dead. The chimney in Kazue's house fell in, sending soot all over the kitchen. Kazue, her nine siblings, and their parents hurriedly dressed and walked to a nearby hill, where they would be safer. They sat there for two and a half days, watching the city burn.

Kazue helped her mother turn their church into a makeshift hospital. Kazue cared for the wounded and translated medical advice for Japanese American women. The fires of San Francisco burned a desire in her heart to study medicine.

Kazue studied zoology at Stanford University, but after graduating, she wasn't able to find a job. No one would hire her because she was a Japanese American woman. So, she enrolled in a two-year nursing program at Mary Thompson Women and Children's Hospital in Chicago. But again, no one would give her a job. In many parts of the United States, hospitals weren't hiring Japanese nurses. It was unheard of to hire them.

Kazue was tired of having nursing jobs go only to white people. She decided that if no one would hire her to become a nurse, she would just have to become a doctor. So, in 1929, she enrolled in Women's Medical College in Philadelphia. She graduated four years later as one of the first Japanese American doctors. She moved back to San Francisco, practiced medicine downtown, and bought a house.

Then, in 1941, another catastrophe turned Kazue's world upside down. Japan, the land of her parents' birth, bombed Pearl Harbor, a U.S. naval base in Hawaii. In response, America declared war on Japan and officially joined World War II.

All of a sudden, Japanese Americans were treated with suspicion. People suspected they would side with Japan, even though they had lived in the United States for many years, or even their entire life. Some Americans mistrusted them so much that President Franklin D. Roosevelt issued an executive order that gave the U.S. army the power to create zones for "enemy aliens." Japanese were called "aliens" because they were seen as foreigners from another country, even though many had been born and raised in the United States. Now that Japan had bombed the United States, they were considered enemies, too.

In 1942, 120,000 Americans with Japanese **ancestry** were ordered to move into 18 internment camps. If someone had immigrated to the United States, had been born there, or even if they had just one great-great-grandparent who was Japanese, they were evacuated. It didn't matter whether they were U.S. citizens or not.

Allowed only two suitcases per person, Kazue and other Japanese Americans packed up what they could, like bedding, kitchen utensils, toiletries, and clothing. They sold or gave away the rest and asked neighbors to watch their homes and businesses.

Kazue was bused to Tanforan, a horse racetrack 12 miles south of San Francisco. It was quickly turned into cramped living quarters for 8,033 evacuees, while more permanent camps were being built. Stables were cleaned and turned into rooms, but the stench remained. Barbed wire surrounded the compound with armed military police patrolling. Families were packed into small apartments with no privacy.

It was here that Kazue was asked to lead the medical team. Besides one other Japanese doctor and some nurses, she was the oldest and most experienced in medicine. After setting up and organizing the hospital, she delivered 50 babies and gave the best care that she could within their rough living quarters. Kazue served at five other internment camps all along the West Coast, earning only around $16 a month.

"EVERYBODY WAS HAPPY TO SEE A JAPANESE WOMAN DOCTOR."

Finally, in the fall of 1943 (two years before America's victory over Japan), Kazue was released from the internment camp. She returned to her home in San Francisco only to find that many of her cherished possessions had been stolen.

But nobody could steal her passion for medicine. She reopened her **private practice** and, for the next 40 years, gave expert medical care to the Asian American community. Even when patients couldn't pay her, she still cared for them.

Dr. Kazue Togasaki blazed her way into the medical field and became one of the first Japanese American woman doctors. She was a leader with a kind and caring heart. The *San Francisco Examiner* named her one of the "Most Distinguished Women of 1970." She lived to the age of 95 and died in 1992. Following in her footsteps, her five younger siblings also went into the medical field.

Because of Dr. Togasaki, many babies born in the Japanese internment camps lived. Her bravery and strong will helped her lead during one of America's most shameful times.

EXPLORE MORE! Visit the Japanese American National Museum in Los Angeles. Or, to learn about what Japanese internment was like, read *So Far from the Sea* by Eve Bunting, about a girl who visits Manzanar War Relocation Center, where her father had been interned and where her grandfather died.

DID YOU KNOW? Dr. Kazue Togasaki delivered over 10,000 babies during her career as a doctor!

Chien-Shiung
WU
{ 1912–1997 }

Dr. Chien-Shiung Wu was a Chinese American **physicist**. She overcame obstacles as an Asian American woman in a mostly male scientific world. She was so successful that male physicists came knocking on her door for help. She worked on a top secret project to end World War II and made new discoveries. She is known as the first lady of physics.

Growing up in China, Chien-Shiung and her two brothers would sit close to their father each night while he read to them about the latest scientific discoveries. He was an engineer, and he wanted all his children to learn science. At the time, girls in China weren't encouraged to study, but her father wanted Chien-Shiung to go to school. So, he started the Mingde Women's Vocational Continuing School for girls.

After graduating from her father's elementary school, Chien-Shiung attended the boarding school Soochow School for Girls. She taught herself math, physics, and chemistry, borrowing friends' textbooks once she'd read all her own. Her favorite subject was physics. In 1929, she graduated high school at the top of her class and was chosen to attend National Central University. But there were no graduate studies in physics in China at this time. If she wanted to continue her education, she would need to go to America.

Chien-Shiung sailed to the United States with plans to attend the University of Michigan. However, when she found out that women weren't allowed at their new student center, she switched to the University of California, Berkeley. There she completed experiments that she would use throughout her life as a physicist. During her time at Berkeley, she married Luke Chia-Liu Yuan.

After graduating, Chien-Shiung wanted to work at the University of California, Berkeley, but they wouldn't hire a woman or an Asian American. Many people on the West Coast didn't trust Asians because they blamed them for Japan's attack on Pearl Harbor. So, Chien-Shiung and Luke moved to the East Coast. Chien-Shiung taught at Smith College, a women's college, while her husband worked in Princeton for the Department of Defense. Soon, she joined him at Princeton as the university's first woman professor.

In 1944, a new opportunity came her way. She joined the top secret **Manhattan Project**, the U.S. military's program to create an **atomic bomb**. Chien-Shiung's experiments and physics research at Berkeley had prepared her for this important project. The bomb was tested in New Mexico in 1945. Soon thereafter, the U.S. military dropped atomic bombs on two cities in Japan, ending World War II.

As World War II ended, a **civil war** was just starting in China. It was too dangerous for Chien-Shiung to visit her family there.

Starting in 1945, Chien-Shiung taught at Columbia University. She stretched the minds of her students and encouraged them to work as hard as she did. She conducted new research, developing a way to measure **nuclear radiation** levels. She also confirmed Italian physicist Dr. Enrico Fermi's 1933 theory of "beta decay"—how a radioactive **atom** becomes more stable.

In 1947, she gave birth to a son named Vincent. She became a U.S. citizen so she could safely raise Vincent in the United States.

"I SINCERELY DOUBT THAT ANY OPEN-MINDED PERSON REALLY BELIEVES IN THE FAULTY NOTION THAT WOMEN HAVE NO INTELLECTUAL CAPACITY FOR SCIENCE AND TECHNOLOGY."

In 1956, two physicists named Dr. Tsung-Dao Lee and Dr. Chen Ning Yang wanted Chien-Shiung to test a physics law called the "conservation of parity." This law stated that both sides of an atom will act the same, with behavior on the left side of the atom mirroring the action of the right side. But no one had been able to prove or disprove it. These two physicists thought this accepted theory might actually be incorrect.

Chien-Shiung found a lab to cool the atoms down to –460 degrees Fahrenheit, where all motion stops. Then, using a **magnetic field**, she observed what happened to the atoms. She discovered that they did *not* mirror each other. Chien-Shiung's experiment disproved a law of physics. The *New York Times* and *Time Magazine* featured her work. However, happiness fizzled into disappointment. Tsung-Dao Lee and Chen Ning Yang received the Nobel Prize for coming up with the theory—but it was Chien-Shiung who had done all of the work!

Even though she didn't get the credit she deserved, Chien-Shiung kept working. She went on to prove two other laws of physics and helped doctors learn how to treat a disease called **sickle cell anemia**.

And though she never won the Nobel Prize, she received many other awards. In 1959, she received the Achievement Award from the American Association of University Women. In 1965, she won the Chi-Tsin Achievement Award in Taiwan. In 1969, she was named an honorary **fellow** at the Royal Society of Edinburgh. In 1973, she received the Michael I. Pupin Professor of Physics award at Columbia. *Industrial Research Magazine* named her scientist of the year in 1974. President Gerald Ford awarded her the National

Medal of Science, the highest science award in the United States.

By the time it was finally safe for Chien-Shiung to visit China, her uncle and younger brother had been killed, and her parents' gravesites had been ruined. She traveled to Mingde School, where her journey began, in commemoration of what would have been her father's 100th birthday. She donated money to the school for scholarships and teachers. In 1992, the Chinese government opened a lab and museum in her honor. Hardworking Chien-Shiung died at age 84.

To this day, Dr. Chien-Shiung Wu remains a role model. She lectured on physics around the world. She proved and disproved theories. She helped end World War II and still had time to care for each of her students. During a time when women were looked down upon in science, she showed the world what a woman could do.

EXPLORE MORE! To learn about more women in science, read *Bold Women in Science* by Danni Washington. To learn about and interact with physics models, visit the L.R. Ingersoll Physics Museum in Madison, Wisconsin.

DID YOU KNOW? In 1990, an asteroid was named in Chien-Shiung Wu's honor.

Isabella Aiona
ABBOTT
{ 1919–2010 }

D r. Isabella Aiona Abbott was the first native Hawaiian woman to receive a **doctorate** in science. Studying plants, she became an expert in marine **algae** of the central Pacific coast of the United States. She is called the first lady of *limu*, the Hawaiian word for seaweed. Isabella—or Izzie, for short—discovered many types of algae.

Isabella Kauakea Yau Yung Aiona was born in Maui. Her mother was a native Hawaiian, and her father was a Chinese immigrant. Izzie's Hawaiian name means "white rain of Kana," after the white mist along the ocean shore. She and her seven brothers grew up surrounded by the sea.

When she was young, she and her brother Frank would walk on the beaches with their mother, but not to swim, or play, or build sandcastles. Instead, they collected seaweed. Waves rushed in and dropped seaweed on the sandy beaches. She and Frank scooped it up in their arms.

Near her grandmother's house on the beach, her mother taught Izzie the Hawaiian names of 70 kinds of edible seaweed. Every mother and aunt knew the names for each plant. Izzie's mom showed her traditional ways of using it and cooking it. Seaweed could be cleaned, pounded, and salted. It could be eaten raw, marinated, or deep-fried. Her mother's knowledge of plants fascinated Izzie.

When Izzie was in seventh grade at an all-girls school, she and her classmates tended flower gardens. Latin names labeled each kind of flower. The principal, Ms. Schaeffer, taught Izzie that Latin names have meanings, just like her Hawaiian name had a meaning. Later, Izzie would give Latin names to algae.

Izzie loved learning about plants. She got a degree in **botany**, the study of plants, at the University of Hawaii in 1941. Then she got her master's degree in 1942 from the University of Michigan. And in 1950, she graduated from the University of California, Berkeley, becoming the first native Hawaiian woman to get her doctorate in science. Of course, it was in botany!

In addition to plants, Izzie also grew her own family. She married Donald Putnam Abbott, a zoologist, and gave birth to a daughter named Annie. During this time, there weren't many jobs for women with doctorates. Izzie stayed home with their daughter for 10 years. She created recipes using seaweed and wrote a book. Discovering new plants, like algae, was a game to her. She would guess a plant's **species** and study it under a microscope to see if she was correct. For new plants, she would name them, find out their history, and then classify them.

"HAWAIIAN CULTURE IS UNBELIEVABLY SOPHISTICATED."

In 1960, Izzie started teaching at Stanford University as their first woman professor in biology. She was also the school's first person of color to become a biology professor. Because she grew up with seven brothers, being the only woman in this department didn't bother her. She taught at Stanford for 30 years.

Izzie's love for seaweed made it into many dishes that she brought to potlucks and picnics. Would you eat *nereocystis* cake, or kelp cake? This delicious creation was gobbled up quickly. She also got the other staff and students involved in making kelp pickles. They soaked the seaweed until it became crispy. Izzie's expertise in cooking seaweed was featured in *Gourmet* magazine in 1987.

In 1976, Izzie wrote the book *Marine Algae of California*, which included over 700 scientific descriptions of algae. She went on to write seven other books and more than 150 scientific papers.

In 1982, she retired from Stanford and moved back to Hawaii to teach at the University of Hawaii. She took students to the beaches, where she taught them her love of seaweed. Her favorite seaweed was *Liagora*, an inedible seaweed that her mother would not approve of.

Another seaweed in Hawaii that was special to Izzie was *limu kala*. *Kala* means to forgive but also means spiny. In the Hawaiian culture, at a family meeting, family members would hold these spiny brown algae in their hands to symbolize that they would forgive and love each other.

Dr. Isabella Aiona Abbott discovered and named over 200 species of algae. In 1969, she received the Darbaker Prize. In 1993, she was awarded the Charles Reed Bishop Medal. In 1997, she received the Gilbert Morgan Smith Medal, the highest award in marine biology from the National Academy of Sciences. In 2005, Honpa Hongwanji Mission of Hawaii named her a "living treasure of Hawai'i." And she received the Lifetime Achievement Award from the Hawaii Department of Land and Natural Resources.

Izzie also had the privilege of naming a National Oceanic Atmospheric Administration (NOAA) research ship. She called it the *Hi'ialakai*, after the reef fishes that poke around in the water. She also named a type of seaweed after the captain of the *Hi'ialakai*. Izzie was still serving on various committees and museum boards until close to her death at age 90 in 2010.

Students still remember Izzie when they read her books and study algae. Her tremendous work helped preserve native Hawaiian plant life. In 2016, the professor of botany at the University of Hawaii led students on a reef cleanup to remove **invasive** algae in Dr. Abbott's honor. Her legacy continues to flourish, just like the algae in the sea.

YOU CAN TRY SOME EDIBLE SEAWEED! At many Asian or international grocery stores, and even some American supermarkets, you can find healthy, crispy seaweed snacks.

DID YOU KNOW? Dr. Isabella Abbott has several types of algae named after her, including *Abbottella*, or Little Abbott, a type of red algae.

Jacqueline
WHANG-PENG
{ 1932– }

Dr. Jacqueline Whang-Peng is a Taiwanese American **genetic oncologist**. She treats and researches cancer. She made an important discovery proving that cancer is caused by changes in the **chromosomes** of cells. She was the first woman surgeon in Taiwan and is called "the Mother of Oncology" in Taiwan.

Jacqueline was born in China in 1932. As a girl with boundless energy, she loved tap dancing. But after her brother died of asthma, she put all that energy into studying to be a doctor.

In 1949, when Jacqueline was 16 years old, China became a **communist** country. The government would now own all property and control people's lives. To escape the upheaval, Jacqueline sailed for two days with her brothers, sisters, and mother to freedom on the island of Taiwan. She attended Medical College of Taiwan University and graduated in 1956. She became Taiwan's first woman surgeon, for which she was awarded the National Outstanding Female Youth Award in 1968.

In 1957, Jacqueline went to the United States to carry out her dream of becoming a surgeon. She became a resident intern at New England Hospital in Boston. After she finished her residency, Tufts University Affiliated Hospital offered her a job. But when her new employer found out she wanted to start work one week later because she was getting married, they took away the job offer.

Jacqueline didn't let this heartbreak set her back. She got a job in cancer research at the National Institutes of Health. Little did she know this would become her life's work.

She stayed at the institute from 1960 to 1993. While there, she discovered that changes in chromosomes caused cancer. Chromosomes are the parts in cells that determine what your body looks like, such as what color your eyes and hair are. People with cancer had chromosomes that were broken, had moved, or even had disappeared. For this discovery, in 1972, Jacqueline became the first woman *and* the first person born outside the United States to win the Arthur S. Flemming Award for outstanding work by a government employee.

Jacqueline lived in the United States for more than 30 years and even became a U.S. citizen. She was the director of the Public Health Section and Chief of Cytogenetic Oncology at the National Cancer Institute.

Being a wife and mother to four children plus being a doctor was tough. Thankfully, her family supported her and helped her along the way.

She loved her job at the institute, but her heart was in Taiwan. She knew that cancer was one of the leading causes of death in Taiwan, where they didn't have access to all the medicines and cancer doctors that the U.S. did. Wealthy Taiwanese could fly overseas for cancer treatments. But the poor were left to die.

Many Taiwanese were dying of nose and throat, liver, and stomach cancers. These were not common in the United States. So, Jacqueline decided to do something about it. She would return to Taiwan and offer her expertise. On January 1, 1994, she left her husband, two sons, and two daughters to embark on a mission to save lives.

"WITH CONTINUOUS HARD WORK, SUPPORT FROM OTHERS AND A BIT OF LUCK, I TRUST THAT THERE WILL BE MORE SUCCESSFUL WOMEN SCIENTISTS IN [TAIWAN]."

In Taiwan, Jacqueline led a team of researchers and worked closely with another American cancer expert, Dr. Paul Carbone. She trained doctors, nurses, and researchers to more effectively treat cancer. She founded the Formosa Cancer Foundation with the mission of preventing cancer, and she became the director of Taiwan's cancer institute. In 2008, Jacqueline was awarded the very first L'Oreal Taiwan Outstanding Woman Scientist Award.

Today, Jacqueline works at the Taipei Municipal Wanfang Hospital. She's written more than 450 publications and continues to lead research. She's 90 years old, but she doesn't have time to be old. She sees cancer patients along with researching and leading others in the medical profession.

She attributes her continued health and energy to eating lots of healthy fruits and vegetables, carrying around a big bag of reports and research to exercise her hands and legs, and trying to get enough sleep.

Dr. Jacqueline Whang-Peng pioneered cancer research and development. Her caring heart and abundance of energy transformed, and continues to transform, lives. She led medical teams in both the United States and Taiwan. And most of all, she continues adding to her legacy by encouraging women to enter the science field.

EXPLORE MORE! Jacqueline encourages people to eat at least five fruits and vegetables a day. Plan a meal for your day that includes lots of fruits and vegetables.

DID YOU KNOW? Dr. Jacqueline Whang-Peng encouraged her two daughters to become doctors. One is a surgeon, and the other is a dermatologist, which means skin doctor.

Roseli
OCAMPO-FRIEDMANN
{ 1937–2005 }

D r. Roseli Ocampo-Friedmann was a Filipino American microbiologist and botanist. She studied teeny-tiny creatures, known as **microorganisms**, like bacteria and algae. Her work with these microorganisms caught the attention of **NASA**. The microorganisms she found grew in extreme places. Her study led the way for new thinking about life on Mars.

Roseli Ocampo was born on November 23, 1937, in Manila, Philippines. She got a degree in botany from the University of Philippines in 1958 and received a master's degree at Hebrew University in Israel in 1966. After working for the National Institute of Science and Technology in the Philippines, she went to Florida State University to join Dr. Imre Friedmann, a Hungarian professor.

In 1973, she received her doctorate in botany, and the following year she married Dr. Friedmann. She became a professor at Florida A&M University and Florida State University. She also worked as a scientific consultant for the Search for Extraterrestrial Intelligence (SETI) Institute.

Roseli and her husband traveled the world to extreme places to look for signs of life where it seemed like no life could survive. Extreme places are those with extraordinarily hot deserts, icy-cold poles, boiling water, or high air pressure. These are places where humans (and more of the plants and animals we know) could never live. Roseli and Imre thought perhaps microorganisms *could* live in these extreme environments.

While in Jerusalem, they often went to the Negev Desert. Roseli and Imre wondered if seaweed such as algae could grow there. They searched for life in the soil. But they found nothing. One day, an oil geologist brought them a desert rock with something green inside. Could it be? They scraped some off and studied it under a microscope. It was algae! Now Roseli and Imre knew tiny life could grow inside rocks.

Rocks have empty spaces that can hold water. Light can shine into cracks and clear parts. With water and light, algae can make food and survive. Now Roseli and Imre knew where to look. They and their team broke open rock after rock and found algae living in many of them. Their searches for life in extreme places took them to the Gobi Desert in Mongolia, the Atacama Desert in Chile, the frozen lands of Siberia, the high mountains, and the deep sea.

But there was one extreme place they hadn't gone yet—Antarctica. This continent isn't just deep snow and ice. Antarctica is actually a desert. It doesn't get much rain or snow. There are no trees or bushes. And because it's the coldest place on Earth, the little rain or snow that *does* fall builds up over time. For all these reasons, it's very hard for life to survive in Antarctica. But could there be microorganisms? Roseli and Imre had found them in Siberia, drilling 3,000 feet in frozen soil. So, they thought they could try again in Antarctica.

There was just one problem: No one would pay for their research trip.

But Roseli and Imre had an idea. NASA sends scientists to Antarctica because it has some of the same conditions as the planet Mars. Both are extremely cold and dry. NASA scientists who would be manning the *Viking 1* rocket to Mars were going to head to Antarctica first to train. Imre met one of *Viking 1*'s leading scientists, Wolf Vishniac. Imre showed him the rocks from the Negev Desert. Dr. Vishniac agreed to look for rocks in Antarctica.

Roseli and Imre were so excited. If they couldn't go to Antarctica themselves, this would be the next best thing. In 1973, Dr. Vishniac and another geologist began experiments on a mountainous area. However, Dr. Vishniac died soon after he left camp. Roseli and Imre were devastated, convinced they would never know if Dr. Vishniac had found anything for them.

But then, two months later, a letter arrived from Dr. Vishniac's wife. She had a collection of rocks from Antarctica for them. When Roseli and Imre broke open a small sandstone only two inches long in their lab, they discovered bacteria. They'd been right: Microorganisms could live in Antarctica! They named this bacteria cryptoendolith. *Crypto* means hidden. *Endolith* means inside rocks. Roseli grew a **colony** of this new bacteria in her lab. Instead of having a "green thumb," people said she had a "blue-green thumb," because of the bluish color in the algae.

Thanks to these findings, they received money to begin research. They went on 17 trips to McMurdo Station in Antarctica. Helicopters flew them over snowy mountains to the frozen, barren landscape. They left behind instruments to record data in rocks and returned on future trips to check on the results.

On July 20, 1976, NASA's *Viking 1* rocket flew to Mars. The mission scientists didn't find any signs of life, and they said life couldn't survive the planet's conditions. But these scientists hadn't heard about the Friedmanns' discovery. If microorganisms could live inside rocks in Antarctica, then maybe they could live on Mars, too.

A year later, the Friedmanns got a phone call. Scientists at NASA had read their paper. NASA and the National Science Foundation wanted permission to talk about their research and discovery on the news. Of course they said yes.

Perhaps there *were* signs of life on Mars and scientists had simply been looking in the wrong places. Imre suggested that they look in Martian rocks.

One evening in 1978, Roseli and Imre sat down to dinner and turned on the news, like they always did. News anchor Walter Cronkite talked about possible life on Mars. He said that algae or bacteria could be present in the rocks. Roseli nearly dropped her silverware as she realized that he was talking about her research!

In 1996, fossils or something similar to fossilized microbes were found in Martian **meteorites** discovered in Antarctica. Since then, NASA has sent vehicles to Mars to find signs of life. The latest vehicle sent was the *Perseverance* rover in 2020. The search for life continues today, now beneath the surface of Mars, thanks to Roseli and Imre's work.

"THE WORK STARTED BY IMRE AND ROSELI FRIEDMANN IS VERY IMPORTANT FOR SEARCHING [FOR] LIFE ON MARS."

—Daniela Billi, *researcher and professor of biology at the University of Rome*

Roseli's research and discovery earned her the National Science Foundation's Antarctica Service Medal in 1981. She and Imre collected over 1,000 types of microorganisms from extreme environments before Roseli died in 2005 of Parkinson's disease.

EXPLORE MORE! Do you think there is life on Mars? Read books such as *Mars Missions: A Space Discovery Guide* by Buffy Silverman to learn about the red planet.

DID YOU KNOW? Friedmann Peak, in the Darwin Mountains of Antarctica, is named after Roseli. This is one of many places where she discovered microorganisms.

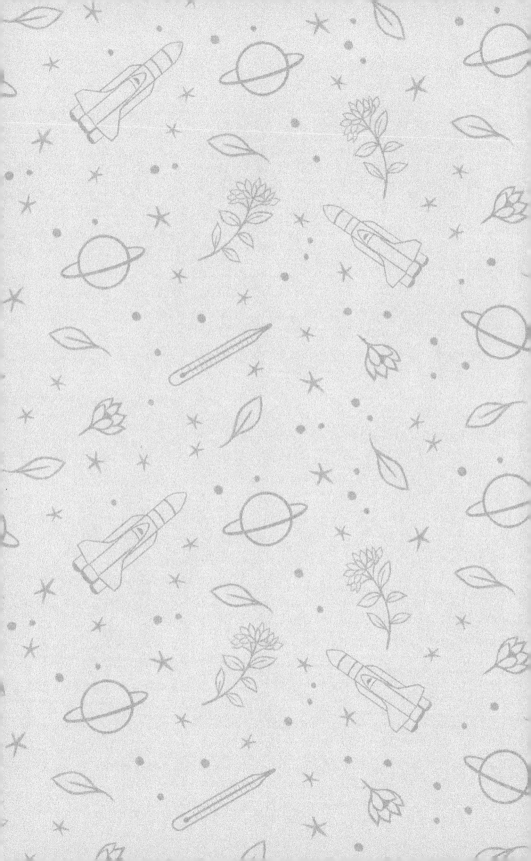

Angelita
CASTRO-KELLY
{ 1942–2015 }

Angelita Castro-Kelly was a Filipino American mathematician and physicist. She took to the stars and paved a new path for women. Angelita was the first woman Mission Operations Manager at NASA. She was a great leader who helped develop the Earth Observing System.

Angelita grew up in Manila in the Philippines. Her family had high hopes for her. Her father was a medical doctor killed in World War II before she was old enough to know him. Her mother was a pharmacist. Her mother and her grandmother wanted her to become a doctor like her father. Angelita's five older siblings became doctors, ambassadors, lawyers, and professors. Angelita wanted to be successful, too. She decided to study math and physics at the University of Santo Tomas in Manila. She graduated with the highest honors in 1962.

After graduating, she went to the United States. She studied at the University of Maryland and got her master's degree in physics. Being in a new country was hard at first. Angelita wasn't used to being around people of different faiths and cultures. Thankfully, her mother and two of her siblings had also moved to the United States and lived close by.

In addition to the challenge of being from another country, she was also outnumbered as a woman in graduate school. In fact, the physics building only had one restroom for women among all four floors. Her strong Christian faith got her through difficult times. She eventually married physicist Dr. Francis Kelly and had three children.

Angelita decided she didn't want to be a doctor. Doctors trained using dead bodies, and she was scared of corpses. She'd rather be a professor. But while she was job hunting, she heard NASA was hiring. The first step was passing a math test. Easy!

Angelita had thought that NASA was only about rockets, but she quickly learned that there was much more to space science. She worked at Goddard Space Flight Center in Maryland. Angelita started as a project manager for the Shuttle/Spacelab Data Processing Facility. She had this job for 12 years. She learned how to interact and negotiate with people at other NASA centers and with space personnel in other countries. This prepared her for her next great work.

In 1990, she became the first woman Mission Operations Manager (MOM) for NASA's Earth Observing System (EOS). The EOS is a collection of unmanned **satellites** that orbit Earth. Each satellite carries instruments that can take pictures and measurements of the clouds, atmosphere, water vapor, gases, tiny air **particles**, Earth's surface, and the ocean. Viewing Earth from space allows NASA to see how the land, water, and atmosphere all work together. It was Angelita's team's job to oversee and analyze the data.

"THE INITIAL CHALLENGE WAS TO SHOW [MEN] THAT I WAS JUST AS CAPABLE AS THEY WERE TO DO THE JOB. THE TRUST AND RESPECT CAME ONCE THEY SAW THAT I COULD CONTRIBUTE TO THE SUCCESS OF THE MISSION."

As the MOM, Angelita was a bridge between engineers and scientists, between ground system developers and international partners in other countries. Her vast knowledge and excellent communication skills earned her respect from her peers. She further developed and organized the EOS, turning it into a more sophisticated system that would become the basis for more missions. She represented NASA at international meetings and kept everything running smoothly.

Angelita also became the Earth Science Constellation Manager. She met with international teams to make sure the satellites launched by all countries were operated safely and followed guidelines. Sometimes she was the only woman in the room at these meetings. Most men were polite, but some were not at first.

Because of Angelita's hard work, Filipino president Fidel Ramos awarded her the Presidential Award, *Pamana ng Bayan*, for Science and Technology. She was named one of the University of Santo Tomas's 10 Outstanding Thomasian Alumni for Science and Technology.

Angelita offered tips for being successful. First, develop strong communication skills, both verbal and written. Second, be willing to get the job done no matter what. Third, don't do only the required work. Go above and beyond. Fourth, be flexible.

She practiced what she preached. NASA awarded her the Exceptional Service Medal, the Graduate School of Frontier Sciences (GSFS) Exceptional Performance Award, the Flight Project's "Mission Impossible" Award, and the NASA Honor Award and Exceptional Achievement Medal. Her favorite was the Astronauts' Manned Flight Snoopy Award. In the *Peanuts* comics, Snoopy liked to fly and was one of NASA's mascots. Because of Angelita's work on the shuttle program, an astronaut presented her the award.

Filipino values also helped Angelita succeed. She honored God and family. Being honest, hardworking, and determined were of utmost importance to her.

She never forgot to pray. She said, "Whatever success I have today is from God, who gave me the grace of an education, and who gave me a wonderful family and a loving husband."

Angelita Castro-Kelly was a great role model for girls and Asian Americans. She was the director for Goddard Space Flight Center's Summer Institute in Science and Technology for Jr. High Girls. She led committees at her work for Asian and Pacific American employees. In so many ways, Angelita reached for the stars.

EXPLORE MORE! Visit a local observatory to learn more about space. An observatory is a place with a powerful telescope to view stars, planets, and more.

DID YOU KNOW? Angelita's nickname was "the MOM." Prior to her, all MOMs at NASA were men.

Joan
BLOCK
{ Circa 1958- }

J oan Block is a Korean American nurse from Pennsylvania. She is a leader in **hepatitis B** research. She and her husband started the Hepatitis B Foundation to help patients with the disease and to find a cure. Joan's work is especially important to the Asian American community, because more than half of all Americans who get this disease are of Asian heritage.

Joan was born in Korea and was adopted by a white American family in Pennsylvania. There weren't many Asian children in the small city of Lancaster. Joan often felt different. When she moved to the big city of Philadelphia, she saw a lot of people who looked like her. Exploring Philadelphia's Chinatown and seeing other Asians made Joan proud of her heritage.

Joan went to Goshen College in Indiana and studied biology. Then she studied nursing at Thomas Jefferson University in Pennsylvania. She worked at a restaurant to pay for her education. While waitressing, she met the man who would later become her husband, Dr. Timothy Block. They married in 1987. Joan has since been a nurse for children with cancer and adults with heart problems, and she has even taught nursing classes.

"I NEVER CONSIDERED MYSELF KOREAN AMERICAN GROWING UP BECAUSE I WAS STRUGGLING ALWAYS AS AN ASIAN IN A WHITE WORLD. NOW, I FEEL PRIDE IN IT."

One day in 1987, when she was 29 years old, Joan went to the doctor for a checkup. The doctor suggested she get tested for hepatitis B because she had high levels of protein in her liver.

Hepatitis B is a liver infection caused by something called the B virus, which attacks and injures the liver. It's carried through the blood and infected bodily fluids. Every year one million people die from the disease.

Joan was devastated when she received the news that she did indeed have hepatitis B. She said she felt like she'd been kicked in the stomach. As a nurse, she knew the disease could be fatal. Many hepatitis B patients died of liver failure or liver cancer. When she worked with them at the hospital, she had to wear protective clothing such as a gown, gloves, and a mask because the patients were so contagious. She wondered how many years she had left to live.

When her employers at the hospital discovered she had the disease, they suspended her. They didn't know what to do with workers infected with hepatitis B. And because mothers could pass the disease to their children at birth, her child was kicked out of day care.

Eventually, after a rough six months, she did get her job back, and her child returned to day care. Meanwhile, Joan and her husband looked for information about hepatitis B. At this time, there was no Internet. There was no support for patients with this disease. There were no treatments or cure either. They had nowhere to turn except to medical books in the library.

But Joan and her husband didn't let that stop them. If there was no support, they would start something themselves. Others like them needed help, too. Tim was a research scientist who studied viruses. He decided to change his focus to hepatitis B and search for a cure. Even the World Health Organization said that hepatitis B was one of the top 10 diseases to eliminate.

Joan and Tim talked with close friends, Paul and Jan Witte. Together, they created the first nonprofit foundation to help people with hepatitis B. This organization started at the kitchen table, and now it is internationally recognized and has 50 scientists looking for a cure.

Through the foundation, Joan has been able to speak up for other patients with the disease. She doesn't want them to be denied opportunities like she was. In 2013, the Americans with Disabilities Act protected health care workers and students against discrimination. In 2015, Joan was asked to serve on the World Health Organization committee to help manage hepatitis B.

Joan has published widely about hepatitis B and is recognized by the White House and the Centers for Disease Control Foundation for her leadership. Joan encourages wide testing for hepatitis B. Many people don't have symptoms, but they can unknowingly transmit the disease to others through blood and infected bodily fluids. Today people can treat and prevent the disease. There is a vaccine for hepatitis B, and scientists are still looking for a cure.

May is Hepatitis Awareness Month. It's also Asian/Pacific American Heritage Month. Joan is happy that both are highlighted together because hepatitis B affects more people of Asian descent.

Joan only recently shared with the world that she had hepatitis B. She kept it hidden because of fear and shame. She also wanted the foundation to help others, not just her. Joan says, "If more of us can stand up and say without fear or hesitation, 'I have hepatitis B,' then we will indeed contribute significantly to making hepatitis B history!"

Joan received the Women of Distinction Award for nonprofit leadership from the *Philadelphia Business Journal*, the Distinguished Health Leadership Award from Penn Asian Senior Services, and the Distinguished

Advocacy Service Award by the American Association for the Study of Liver Diseases. In 2017, Joan retired as executive director of the Hepatitis B Foundation, but she still volunteers as a nurse at a local free clinic. Joan is a good example of someone who saw a need and led an organization to meet it.

EXPLORE MORE! Look at a health book such as *Human Body! (Knowledge Encyclopedia)* by the Smithsonian Institution to learn about what the liver looks like and its function in the body. Think about what diseases or health concerns affect people today. How could you make a difference?

DID YOU KNOW? Liver cancer is the fifth-deadliest cancer in the world.

Josephine
JUE
{ 1946- }

Josephine Jue is a Chinese American computer programmer and mathematician. She was the first Asian American woman to work at NASA. She is best known for her work with computer software that helped land the Apollo space rocket on the moon.

Born in Vance, Mississippi, in 1946, Josephine lived among a growing Chinese population along the Mississippi Delta. Her parents immigrated from China like many others seeking better opportunities. Her mother had no schooling because, back then, people in China didn't believe girls needed an education. Her father only attended school until third grade.

In the latter 1800s and early 1900s in the United States, cotton plantation owners hired laborers from China to work the fields. Enslaved people were being set free, so plantation owners were looking for other workers they could underpay. Eventually, many of these Mississippi Delta Chinese people left farming and turned to the grocery store business. Hundreds of small grocery stores opened up, selling mostly to the Black community.

Josephine's parents were part of this growth of Chinese Americans in the grocery business. They left Mississippi and set up their first grocery store, Far East Grocery, on the north side of Houston, Texas. In 1949, they opened a second store. Josephine and her siblings lived in the house attached to the store. She helped her parents by unpacking boxes of products and placing the items on shelves. She swept and made the place look tidy.

Josephine grew up learning English and speaks little Chinese. Even Chinese New Year customs are foreign to her because her parents often didn't celebrate the holidays of their homeland. Josephine attended the University of Houston and got a degree in mathematics. And as more Chinese Americans came to the Houston area, she met her husband, Vic Jue. They had three children, twin sons and a daughter.

In 1963, Josephine got a job at NASA's Johnson Space Center in Houston as a mathematician. During the time of the **Civil Rights Movement** in America, NASA broke racial barriers by hiring people of different races, ethnicities, and genders. Josephine was one of eight women hired by NASA. She was the first Asian American woman they had ever hired. Using her expertise in math, she wrote computer programs for space shuttle projects. She is best known for the work she did on *Apollo 11*, the first manned mission to the moon.

On July 16, 1969, astronauts Neil Armstrong, Michael Collins, and Buzz Aldrin blasted into space aboard the *Apollo 11* spacecraft. President John F. Kennedy had said in 1961 that America would perform a lunar landing. But without Josephine, that landing wouldn't have been possible. She worked on the computer language for the flight software called HAL/S (High-order Assembly Language/Shuttle). She changed code into language the computers could read.

On July 20, around 650 million people sat in front of their TV sets and radios, watching and listening as history was being made. Armstrong stepped on the moon and said the famous words "That's one small step for man, one giant leap for mankind."

Not only was it a giant leap for mankind, but it was a giant leap for NASA's software. There could be no mistakes on this mission, or the astronauts could die. This was the first time humans walked on the moon. And this was the first time computer software ran on the moon. Josephine and other women who worked with her made this possible.

"WOMEN WERE AN INTEGRAL PART OF THE TEAM THAT HELPED PUT ASTRONAUTS ON THE MOON."

In 1975, Josephine became the chief of NASA's Software Engineering Laboratory. She worked on plans and procedures for the maintenance of the HAL/S space shuttle software and for the hundreds of ground-based computers. She developed software and made sure it worked. NASA could count on Josephine.

Josephine stayed with NASA for 37 years. She said it was a good place to work because they gave her a fair salary and a reasonable amount of time off.

In 2019, the Mississippi Delta Chinese Heritage Museum had an exhibition on Chinese Americans' contributions to the space program and featured a display about Josephine.

Since her retirement, Josephine has been enjoying many hobbies. She likes to play the card game bridge once a month, and she often reads and gardens.

Josephine Jue is an example of an Asian American woman who broke barriers in science, technology, and math. She showed a male-driven organization that they could count on women.

EXPLORE MORE! You might watch the movie *Hidden Figures*, which tells the story of some of the first women who worked at NASA as "human computers."

DID YOU KNOW? Josephine belongs to the Chinese Baptist Church, where she sometimes works in the nursery or teaches.

Fan Rong King Chung
GRAHAM,
AKA FAN CHUNG
{ 1949– }

D r. Fan Chung is a Taiwanese American mathematician. She is a leading expert in special areas of math such as **combinatorics**. She was the first woman professor at the University of Pennsylvania to receive **tenure**, a high academic honor. She is an excellent leader and dedicated scholar.

Fan Rong King Chung was born in Taiwan in 1949. Her favorite class in middle school was **geometry**. Fan's father, an engineer, told her that she should study science, but that studying math was a good foundation.

Fan thought so, too. She was great with numbers. She graduated from National Taiwan University with a degree in mathematics in 1970. One of her favorite kinds of math was combinatorics, which means finding all the connections and combinations to number problems.

Fan's mother was a high school teacher. Many women at the time did not work, but Fan thought if her mother could have her own career, so could she.

So, Fan went to the United States to study math at the University of Pennsylvania. Her mathematics professor was very impressed with her performance on her entry exam. She scored higher than anyone in the class. He gave her a book and asked her to read one of the math chapters. When they met the following week, she told him she could solve one of the problems better than the author of the math book. And she did! To her, it was like putting a puzzle together. In 1972, Fan graduated with her master's degree in math.

"IF YOU ARE GOOD AT SOMETHING, AND REALLY HAVE IT SOLID, THEN YOU CAN DEVELOP FROM THERE. AND NO ONE KNOWS EVERYTHING— SO DON'T BE INTIMIDATED!"

Fan thought about math all the time. She got married and continued learning new things about math. She had her first baby while studying for her doctorate. In 1974, she graduated with her PhD, also from the University of Pennsylvania. She went to work at Bell Laboratories, a place of research and new technologies for communication. She was a member of the technical staff. There, she worked with many leading mathematicians on all kinds of problems. She collaborated with others and wrote math papers. She enjoyed meeting other mathematicians and learning from them.

Fan dedicated herself to her work. She did math up to the day her second baby was born. She even spent time on her rare vacations writing math papers.

After she and her first husband divorced, Fan married a mathematician, Ron Graham, in 1983. They talked math. They wrote math papers. Math was their life.

Fan got promoted at her job and became the research manager at Bell. For seven years, she supervised mathematicians, read their research papers, and wrote reports. She moved up again, this time to be a division manager for four years. But to Fan, the impressive job titles weren't the most important thing. She wanted to earn people's respect through her knowledge of mathematics, not just because she was their boss.

In 1989, Fan became a visiting professor at Princeton University. And the following year, she was chosen to be a fellow at Harvard University. She gave presentations in Maine and at the International Congress of Mathematicians in Switzerland in 1994. She quit her job at Bell and spent a year at the Institute for Advanced Study at Princeton.

In 1995, she returned to the University of Pennsylvania, this time as a professor of math and computer science. After three years, she moved to the University of California San Diego to became a professor of math, computer science, and engineering.

Fan left numerous marks on the math world through her 300 publications, including three books. She co-wrote one of her books with her husband. This book highlighted the work of another famous mathematician, Paul Erdős, a Hungarian. They were friends with Paul and often invited him to their house. Paul gave Fan math problems he picked up from places he traveled, and she'd solve them. He planted math seeds in her brain, and she made them grow.

Fan was also an editor. She edited 17 math journals. She even started her own journal, *Internet Mathematics*. Her knowledge of math helped improve computers.

Fan received six major awards and honors. She received the Allendoerfer Award in 1990 from the Mathematical Association of America. In 1998, she became a member of the American Academy of Arts and Sciences. She received the Euler Medal from the Institute of Combinatorics. She was a fellow of the American Association for the Advancement of Science and a fellow of the American Mathematical Society. In 2016, she was selected for Academia Sinica, the highest honor for scholars in Taiwan.

Even though she retired in 2016, Fan still mentors part-time as a research professor. Because she received lots of help when she was a student, she wants to provide that same benefit to other students.

When Fan isn't doing math, she's busy pursuing her hobbies. She plays a Chinese harp called a *guzheng*, performs traditional Chinese dances, and works in her yard.

Fan continues to pave the way for women to stick with their work, even when it gets hard, and join the field of mathematics.

EXPLORE MORE! To learn about Paul Erdős, read *The Boy Who Loved Math: The Improbable Life of Paul Erdős* by Deborah Heiligman. If you look closely at the pictures, you'll see an illustration of Fan and her husband, Ron.

DID YOU KNOW? Dr. Fan Chung paints seascapes and portraits of mathematicians who influenced her. She sees connections between math and watercolor painting.

Kalpana
CHAWLA
{ 1962–2003 }

D r. Kalpana Chawla was an Indian American astronaut and engineer. She was the first Indian-born woman to fly to space and the second Indian to fly to space. She made many contributions to space science and logged in many hours of flying.

Kalpana was born in India in 1962. On very hot nights, she and her family slept on the rooftop of their house. Kalpana gazed at the twinkling stars and vowed that, someday, she would fly among them.

Roar! Zoom! Airplanes and gliders flew overhead. Not far from her house was the city's flying club. Another plane swooped by. Kalpana waved to the pilot. Then she and her brother raced on their bikes to see where the planes landed. She got permission to go for a ride in an airplane. She was four years old, and that was her first time in the air.

When Kalpana was growing up in India, school wasn't considered important for girls. But her mother believed that girls should be educated, so she enrolled

Kalpana from a young age. Kalpana was curious and confident.

Until she started school, Kalpana was called by the nickname "Monto." Many families in India would gather together to name a baby, but Kalpana hadn't been given a formal naming ceremony. Her aunt gave her three possibilities for what her name could be. When she started school and her principal asked which name she'd chosen, she said, "Kalpana," which means imagination. And that she did have.

Kalpana loved flying. When her friends drew mountains and rivers, she drew airplanes. In craft classes, she made model planes. And in math class, when the teacher gave an example of something that didn't exist, such as Indian women astronauts, Kalpana spoke up. She said someday they just might.

Her hero was J. R. D. Tata, an Indian aviator who created India's first airline. Kalpana wanted to study about space. Her father wanted her to be a doctor or a teacher instead. But Kalpana was determined.

She attended Punjab Engineering College. Her professors told her there was no future for careers in space travel in India. But Kalpana pressed on and graduated with her degree in aeronautical engineering.

In 1982, she moved to the United States to study at the University of Texas. She graduated in 1982 with her master's degree in **aerospace** engineering. She also met Jean Pierre Harrison, a flight instructor and aviation author. He taught her to fly a plane, and in 1983, they got married. Kalpana got her pilot's license, and together they flew the skies.

In 1986, NASA's space shuttle *Challenger* blew up during a mission. But this did not scare off Kalpana. She still wanted to get to the stars. In 1988, she graduated from the University of Colorado with her doctorate and became a U.S. citizen. She got a job with NASA's Ames Research Center.

In 1993, she was a vice president and research scientist for an aerospace company. In 1994, she was selected as an astronaut candidate. She spent a year in training. Her first flight into space was in November 1997 aboard the shuttle *Columbia*, STS-87. The shuttle carried a Spartan satellite, and Kalpana operated the shuttle's robotic arm to deploy the satellite. She flew 252 orbits around Earth in two weeks.

In 2000, she was selected for another voyage into space as a mission specialist on STS-107. And in 2003, she flew a third time aboard the *Columbia* space shuttle. She performed over 80 experiments and worked on astronaut health and safety issues.

On the morning of February 1, 2003, *Columbia* was supposed to land at Florida's Kennedy Space Center. Kalpana was ready to return to Earth and greet her husband. She had been in space for 30 days, 14 hours, and 54 minutes. However, something was very wrong.

When they had launched, a foam insulation had punched a hole in the heat shield on the wing. Nobody noticed. This system was supposed to protect the spacecraft from overheating when they re-entered Earth's atmosphere. Instead, the spacecraft rolled and lurched. Superheated gases overtook the wing. The shuttle broke up over Texas and Louisiana, with the remains plunging to the ground. All seven astronauts were killed, including Kalpana.

> **"THE PATH FROM DREAMS TO SUCCESS DOES EXIST. MAY YOU HAVE THE VISION TO FIND IT, THE COURAGE TO GET ONTO IT, AND THE PERSEVERANCE TO FOLLOW IT."**

President George W. Bush awarded Kalpana the Congressional Space Medal of Honor after her death. She also received NASA's Space Flight Medal and Distinguished Service Medal. NASA named one of its spacecraft after her. The University of Texas dedicated a display to her, the Kalpana Chawla Memorial, at their college of engineering. Her flight suit, photos, information about her life, and a flag are on display there.

Kalpana had a dream that no children, especially girls, would be deprived of an education. Every year she had paid for two children from India to visit NASA. They stayed with her, and she cooked them Indian food. Kalpana's advice to parents was to listen to their daughters. If they want to study, let them. Make sure they have all they need so they can focus on studying.

When one of Kalpana's high school teachers heard of her death, she said, "She always said she wanted to reach the stars. She went there and beyond."

Dr. Kalpana Chawla's life sets an example for women to follow their dreams, wherever they may lead.

<hr/>

EXPLORE MORE! For more information on the space shuttle *Columbia*, you can read *Columbia Space Shuttle Explosion and Space Exploration* by Tamra Orr.

DID YOU KNOW? Kalpana has a hill on Mars named after her. The NASA Mars Exploration Rover mission named seven peaks in a chain of hills after the seven astronauts who lost their lives. Peak Chawla Hill is one of them.

Alice Min Soo
CHUN
{ 1965– }

Alice Min Soo Chun is a former professor and Korean American inventor who works in **solar energy**. She invented the SolarPuff, a pop-up solar light that is easy to transport and store. This invention is especially helpful in developing nations and in disaster areas where there is no electricity. Alice is a shining light in the world.

Alice grew up in South Korea and later New York. She liked to watch her mother, an artist and textile maker, sew and create with cloth. She liked to watch her father, an architect, design buildings.

Growing up in an all-white community in New York left her with bruises and black eyes from mean kids who bullied her. So, Alice withdrew into her art and imagination. She got out colored squares of paper, folded, creased, and folded some more, until she created a structure. This was origami paper art that her mother had taught her. And it brought her peace.

Alice later took that love for structure and design and got a master's degree in architecture at the University of Pennsylvania. She became a professor at Columbia University, teaching architecture and material technology. She also taught at The New School's Parsons School of Design and lectured at prestigious universities including Harvard, Yale, and MIT.

Alice focused on solar energy, or using energy from the sun. The sun is the most powerful source of energy. And unlike many other forms of energy, it's free, abundant, and doesn't damage Earth. Alice sewed solar panels into fabrics and experimented with ways to create clean energy.

Alice married and had a son named Quinn. Because Quinn had asthma, which is a health condition that makes it hard to breathe, Alice decided to research what caused it. She discovered that, in New York City, one in four children have asthma. Air pollution is one of the triggers, and buildings emit lots of it. Even one light bulb emits 90 pounds of pollution a year.

Alice knew if people changed the way they lived, they could change the climate around them and make it healthier. So, she started experimenting. She turned her classroom into a lab with her college students.

In 2010, an earthquake shook the island of Haiti. One million people lost power. Living on three dollars a day, Haitians had to buy kerosene lamps, which run on oil, to use as lights. Alice knew from her research that two million children die each year from kerosene pollution. It is toxic and deadly.

She wanted to help. In her lab, she worked and worked making hundreds of models, until finally she made a portable light that used solar energy. Thinking back to her days of making origami balloons, she used a folded structure to create the SolarPuff, a cube of solar light. It could charge in the daylight and light the room at night. Made of recyclable materials, it was lightweight and it could pop up and glow.

"A MIGHTY LIGHT THAT WE ARE ALL BORN WITH—IT'S CALLED GENIUS. TAP INTO THAT LIGHT THAT'S IN YOUR MINDS AND IN YOUR HEARTS. STEP BY STEP AND WITH SMALL STEPS AND SMALL ACTS, IN MULTITUDE, WILL MOVE MOUNTAINS."

She applied for a **patent** so no one else could copy her new invention. Then she tried selling it to see if people liked it. She raised enough money to produce her product and found a manufacturer to make it. In 2015, she launched her company, Solight Design Inc. She tested the SolarPuff in Haiti for three years.

One mother in Haiti called it a "gift from God." She couldn't afford glass to go around the kerosene lamp, so her five children were coughing and wheezing from the smoke. But with Alice's SolarPuff, she no longer had to deal with the harmful kerosene.

Alice has taken her invention around the world to disaster areas and places without electricity. In 2017, she went to Puerto Rico after Hurricane Maria devastated the island. Half of the residents had no power. Alice raised $500,000 to give families her solar lights. The mayor of San Juan called it a "cube of hope."

From Haiti to Nigeria to Nepal to the United States, Alice's invention is saving lives. Over one million people have been impacted by it. Not only does it give light to people without electricity, but it also allows **refugees** to travel in dangerous circumstances. Because Alice's invention lights up tent camps, crime has decreased in those areas. Also, children can read at night in places without electricity.

When Alice sees a problem, she invents a solution. During the pandemic of 2020, people wore face masks. However, their mouths were covered and their ears got tired from the mask loops. Alice invented a transparent silicone mask without ear loops that sticks to the face and doesn't hide smiles. She started a new company for it: SEEUS95, Inc.

Alice's achievements include publishing a book about helping devastated communities, receiving the U.S. Patent for Humanity award, and having her inventions on display at the Museum of Modern Art. She's been on TV and podcasts, and has even spoken at the United Nations. And Hillary Clinton, former Secretary of State, included Alice in her book about gutsy women who are doing incredible things for Earth.

Alice says to run a business you must do the research. Understand the problem that your invention will solve. Have grit. Never give up. Use your light to create change in the world.

EXPLORE MORE! You can make your own origami crafts from a book such as *Origami Made Simple: 40 Easy Models with Step-by-Step Instructions* by Russell Wood.

DID YOU KNOW? In August 2021, another deadly earthquake hit Haiti. Alice went there again, to distribute her solar lights and save lives.

Tuyet-Hanh
SCHNELL
{ 1968– }

Tuyet-Hanh Schnell is a Vietnamese American engineer. She's a great leader and mentor to engineers and to women and girls interested in STEM. She has worked for 30 years with Lockheed Martin, an aerospace company. She likes to pay back the kindnesses and mentoring she received when she was in school.

Hanh was born in 1968 in Vietnam, during the height of the **Vietnam War**. Helicopters hovered overhead. Bullets flew through the air. Hanh's family needed to get out of the country. Communists were taking over.

So, in 1975, Hanh's parents got seven-year-old Hanh and her younger brother on a big Lockheed airplane and flew to freedom in the United States. Little did Hanh know that her future would be working for the company that made that plane!

Coming to a new country and learning English was hard. There was no program at Hanh's elementary school to help. Plus, they had arrived with very few belongings. Her parents got jobs and worked hard to support their family in this new land.

Hanh's interest in science started when she was six years old. She took apart a musical bell to see what made it work. Then she put it back together. The summer after 10th grade, she attended a STEM program where she met engineers and scientists. They loved math and science as much as she did. She was impressed with their impact on the world. Hanh decided she wanted to follow in their footsteps. She told her guidance counselor that she wanted to be an engineer.

Hanh was introduced to a girl from her high school who attended Stevens Institute of Technology, so she decided to go to college there. She was determined to get better at English, so she took classes in British and American literature. To get over her shyness, she joined the college choir and theater productions. Hanh found her voice. Along with getting her degree in electrical engineering in 1991, she also started working as an engineer for Lockheed Martin. In 1994, she received her master's degree in systems engineering from Drexel University.

Hanh rose through the ranks at Lockheed Martin. She worked as a software engineer and then became a manager. She designed weapons systems for ships. She managed other engineers and trained them. She became a senior manager and led product teams. As a systems engineer, she saw products grow from idea to reality. She traveled overseas and within the United States, supporting customers. She managed million-dollar projects.

In 2018, she took a new position to grow in her career. Since her company makes combat systems for ships, Hanh's new project was building destroyers for the Japanese Navy. She traveled back and forth from Japan. She says that being Asian helped her adjust to Japanese culture.

Currently, Hanh is a coach for Lockheed Martin. She teaches workshops on software development and project management, trains others, and travels. She's also the mother of two children.

"JOIN CLUBS, TAKE A MINOR, DO COMMUNITY WORK—DO THINGS THAT WILL HELP YOU EXPLORE THE DIFFERENT PIECES OF WHO YOU ARE, AND WHO YOU WILL BECOME."

Hanh is involved in many programs. She is the co-chair of the Rotary and Mission Systems and also the Women's Impact Network. Additionally, she's on the leadership team for the Asian Connections Affinity Group. She likes to see diverse teams working together and understanding one another.

Hanh uses her voice to encourage women and girls to pursue STEM education. At the Society of Women

Engineers, she runs workshops and writes articles to teach women to become excellent engineers. She helped start STEM Gems for girls ages 9 to 12. She is a mentor and encourages girls through workshops. Hanh is a board member of Junior Achievement in New Jersey where she teaches kids how to manage money.

Hanh received the Evening of Stars Award for helping people from different backgrounds work at her company, and for helping the company be more **inclusive** of people from different communities and backgrounds. She also received the Evening of Excellence Team Award.

She said that when she was a child, she learned to listen well to elders and that the information you receive when you listen is a gift. She knows that being a great leader is more about listening to other people's knowledge and needs than it is about talking.

Where she is from in Asia, the family surname goes first and then the individual's first name. Hanh has said this is because in Vietnam the family is more important than the individual. Similarly, the team is bigger than one person. Hanh has always been a team player at Lockheed.

Because Hanh received such wonderful mentorship when she was young, she likes to give back. She does STEM activities with local students. She advises girls to pursue STEM if they like it. She says to keep a diary. Write down your accomplishments. There's no accomplishment too small to note. Look back and see how far you've come and all you've done. Find trustworthy people to give you honest advice about your abilities.

Hanh shows us how important it is to never stop learning and growing. She worked at Lockheed for 20 years and then took on a new position within the company just to learn something new. She's stayed there for long enough to experience all it has to offer.

The little girl from Vietnam who didn't know English now uses her voice and her listening skills to encourage and give back to others.

EXPLORE MORE! Try some engineering projects of your own from the book *Awesome Engineering Activities for Kids: 50+ Exciting STEAM Projects to Design and Build* by Christina Schul.

DID YOU KNOW? Hanh sings in the Moorestown Music Makers and Lockheed Martin's choir, and she leads her church congregation in singing.

computer[1].science,t[2],opportuni
technology}=
{programme
women=[+]
ender:01

Reshma
SAUJANI
{ 1975– }

Reshma Saujani is an Indian American woman who founded Girls Who Code. She advocates for women and girls, especially those of color, to get good jobs in STEM. She is an example of a brave woman who takes risks. She's inspired and influenced over 300,000 girls.

Reshma learned bravery from her parents. In the 1970s, her family was living in Uganda. The government said Asians had to leave the country. So, as refugees, Reshma's parents fled to the United States. Reshma was born in Illinois. Her parents worked hard and taught her to never give up on pursuing her dreams.

However, there weren't many families who looked like hers. Reshma experienced racism and prejudice growing up, especially in middle school, and she didn't like it. So, she decided to do something.

Reshma started Prejudice Reduction Interested Students Movement, or PRISM. She led her first march when she was 12! She wanted to make a difference in the world, to make things better for more people. As a girl, she thought the way to do that was to be perfect. So, she aimed for straight As on her report card. She went to the top schools. She studied political science and speech communications at the University of Illinois at Urbana-Champaign. She got her master's degree in public policy at the John F. Kennedy School of Government at Harvard University in 1999.

But when she applied to Yale University, she got rejected. Not once, not twice, but three times. Eventually, on her fourth try, she was accepted and graduated with a Juris Doctor degree from Yale Law School in 2002.

After graduating from law school, Reshma worked as an attorney and activist. However, she wasn't completely happy. She would cry herself to sleep at night. One day she saw Secretary of State Hillary Clinton speak. Hillary said that if you fail at something, you shouldn't give up. Keep trying.

So, at age 33, Reshma tried to do something brave. She quit her job and used the money she had made to run for Congress. She was the first Indian American woman to do so. But she lost the race. She ran again for another public office and lost that one, too. But in her failure, she learned something about herself. She could be courageous. She could learn from her failures. She didn't have to be perfect to make a positive difference in the world.

While she was visiting schools during her campaign for votes, she noticed a **gender gap** in technology. More boys than girls were taking computing classes. So, Reshma did something about it.

In 2012, she started a company called Girls Who Code. She would inspire girls and equip them with computing skills for the 21st century. Girls in grades 3 through 12 could attend free school clubs, summer programs, and campus programs. They would design and develop websites and apps and learn about technology jobs and women in that field.

Twenty girls signed up for those first classes. Since then, over 300,000 girls have participated, from every state, and even Canada and the United Kingdom.

Reshma says that women use social media and the Internet more than men, and therefore women should build the computers of tomorrow. She's noticed in her classes that most girls create apps that solve big problems, whereas most boys build apps to satisfy immediate desires like acquiring food.

Some of the problems girls in her classes have tried to tackle include lead poisoning, the Zika virus (a virus spread by mosquitoes), cancer, homelessness, and bullying. These girls were able to empathize with others and show they care about what's happening in their homes and communities. They wanted to do something about big problems.

In 2016, only 26 percent of professional computing jobs were held by women. Reshma hopes that more girls enter STEM jobs as a result of Girls Who Code.

That same year, Reshma gave a TED Talk. TED Talks are speeches by experts who have ideas worth spreading. She wanted the world to know that girls need to be taught to be brave, not perfect. She said that most girls are told to smile pretty, get straight As, and avoid risks and failures. But risks and failures are part of finding solutions in coding. Girls Who Code teaches girls to persevere, be courageous, and get comfortable with imperfection.

"WE MUST ELEVATE FEMALE ROLE MODELS—ESPECIALLY [FOR] GIRLS AND WOMEN OF COLOR—IN POP CULTURE, BUSINESS, AND EVERYDAY LIFE."

In 2019, Girls Who Code was awarded Most Innovative Non-Profit by Fast Company. Reshma is listed in *Forbes Magazine* as one of the Most Powerful Women Changing the World and one of the World's Greatest Leaders. Fast Company listed her as one of 100 Most Creative People, and she's in *Fortune* magazine's 40 Under 40 list. Also, she was the winner of the Harold W. McGraw Jr. Prize in Education.

In 2020, during the pandemic, Reshma held a summer virtual program for girls. Five thousand girls built websites and apps to solve problems they faced, including racism. Girls Who Code has a diversity of students, which Reshma says is the "key to innovation."

In 2021, Reshma stepped aside so a new CEO could run her company. She continues to be creative in finding solutions to our world's problems. She wants every girl to have the opportunity to code. She wants them to be brave, not perfect. And as Reshma raises her two children, she also advocates for moms in the workforce. Her hope for the future is that the gender gap in computer programming closes by 2030.

EXPLORE MORE! To learn more about coding, read Reshma Saujani's book *Girls Who Code: Learn to Code and Change the World.*

DID YOU KNOW? Reshma has a journal by her bed where she writes down her thoughts before she goes to sleep at night, especially if she has to give a talk the next day.

Maryam
MIRZAKHANI
{ 1977–2017 }

Maryam Mirzakhani was an Iranian American mathematician. She was the first Iranian woman to win the Fields Medal, the highest honor in mathematics. She has been called the "master of curved space," a child prodigy, and a genius.

Maryam was born in Tehran, Iran, in 1977. Curled up in a chair, she would read every book she could find. She loved writing and making up her own stories. She watched TV shows about famous women like Marie Curie and Helen Keller. They inspired her to do something great in life. Maybe she would be a writer!

During her time at an all-girls elementary school, the war between Iran and Iraq was ending. New opportunities were beginning. Maryam took a placement test and got into a top all-girls middle school. Here she found a lifelong friend, Roya Beheshti. Roya loved stories, too, and together they explored bookstores and bought books.

Roya also liked math. Maryam didn't do that well in math her first year in middle school. Her teacher didn't think she was very good at it either, so Maryam lost interest in the subject. But during her second year of middle school, she received encouragement from her teacher, and her math grades improved.

Maryam and Roya spent more and more time talking and reading about math. They had heard about problem-solving classes at the boys' schools. They wanted similar math classes at their girls' school, too. So, they asked the principal, and she said yes!

By age 17, Maryam made the team for the International Mathematical Olympiad. In 1994, she won a gold medal. And the next year, she won two more gold medals with a perfect score. Maryam was the first girl on Iran's national math team.

In 1999, Maryam received a bachelor's degree in mathematics from Sharif University of Technology in Tehran. She decided to continue her studies in America. She earned her PhD in math from Harvard University in 2004. While at Harvard, she solved two math problems that had never been solved before. Her professors were amazed. She was a research fellow at Princeton University. Then she became a full professor at Stanford University in 2008. She married a computer scientist, Jan Vondrák, also a professor at Stanford.

Maryam studied round surfaces of shapes. She proved math theories about the shortest paths between two points on curved surfaces and found multiple solutions to a problem. She wrote three major papers that were published in top math journals. Big math problems intrigued Maryam.

Maryam would lay huge sheets of paper on the floor to work out her math problems. Math was always visual for her. She'd imagine a picture in her mind and then sketch it out. Drawing shapes, writing lines of formulas, and doodling diagrams made her seem like a painter to her daughter, Anahita. "Oh, Mommy is painting again," Anahita would say.

To Maryam, math was like solving a fun puzzle or connecting the dots in a detective's case. She thought deeply about each problem before trying to solve it. She compared math problems to being lost in a jungle. She used all her knowledge to find her way out.

In 2013, she wrote a paper about how she solved math problems. Because she loved reading books, to her, solving math problems was like writing a novel with different characters. She would get to know the characters really well to solve the problem. Sometimes, Maryam worked quickly. Other times, she worked on a problem for months or years, slowly and intensely.

In 2014, Maryam won the highest award in mathematics, the Fields Medal. It was only given to up to four mathematicians under the age of 40 every four years. Maryam was the first woman and first Iranian to receive it. But getting to the awards ceremony was difficult. Maryam had been diagnosed with breast cancer in 2013 and was receiving chemotherapy treatments.

Still, she flew to Seoul, South Korea, for the International Congress of Mathematicians. She was weak from breast cancer, and so other women helped her and shielded her from the press.

Maryam won other awards as well. She won the Clay Research Award, the American Mathematical Society Blumenthal Award, and the Ruth Lyttle Satter Prize by the American Mathematical Society. She was elected to the French Academy of Sciences, the National Academy of Sciences, and the American Academy of Arts and Sciences.

Maryam liked to listen to other mathematicians and ask them questions. She liked talking with her graduate students helping them further their careers. She generously shared her ideas. She was also an editor for the *Journal of the American Mathematical Society*.

"I WILL BE HAPPY IF [MY WORK] ENCOURAGES YOUNG FEMALE SCIENTISTS AND MATHEMATICIANS."

Cancer took Maryam's life when she was only 40, but her legacy lives on. The Maryam Mirzakhani Prize in Mathematics is a $20,000 prize awarded every two years. Her contributions to higher geometry are often used by mathematicians. Iran's president Hassan Rouhani praised her in one of many tributes people gave when she died. Maryam's passion and joy for math encourages girls and women to this day.

<hr>

EXPLORE MORE! Read the biography *Maryam's Magic: The Story of Mathematician Maryam Mirzakhani* by Megan Reid.

DID YOU KNOW? When Maryam was told she had won the prestigious Fields Medal, she thought it was a joke!

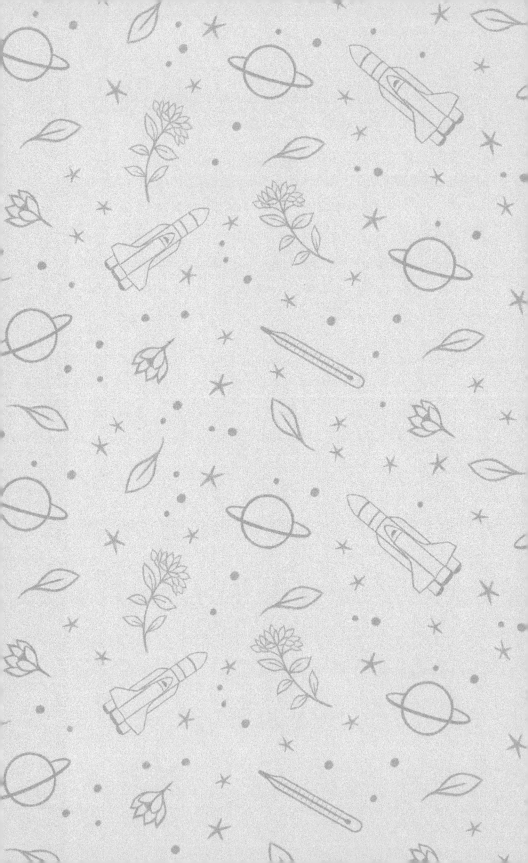

Glossary

advocate: to speak up or give support for someone or something

aerospace: the atmosphere and outer space, and the technology of flight

algae: plants without leaves or stems that grow in or around water

ancestry: family members going many generations back

atom: the smallest unit of matter

atomic bomb: an explosive device with extreme power to destroy through heat, blast, and radioactivity

botany: the science of plants

California Gold Rush: a time in the late 1840s and early 1850s when hundreds of thousands of people migrated to California to mine for gold

chromosomes: parts of cells that include genes, which tell the body how to grow and what to become

Civil Rights Movement: a time of struggle during the 1950s and 1960s when Black people in the United States fought to end racial discrimination and have equal rights

civil war: a war between people in the same country

colony: a group such as bacteria that came from the same cell

combinatorics: an area of math that deals with counting

communist: one who follows a political system in which the government controls and owns all property

doctorate: the highest degree awarded by a graduate school or college (also known as a PhD)

fellow: an advanced student at a university who is paid to study by an organization or business

foundation: an organization that people donate money to in order to help the community or a specific cause

gender gap: the difference between how women and men are treated, particularly in regard to how much they get paid

genetic oncologist: a doctor who studies how cancer spreads in families

geometry: the study of shapes, points, lines, and angles

hepatitis B: a liver disease

inclusive: to be open and include all people in a group

internment camps: prisons where political enemies are housed during a war

internships: positions of training and getting experience for a job

invasive: when a species settles someplace other than its natural habitat

legislation: a law

magnetic field: an area or space around magnetic material within which the force of magnetism acts

Manhattan Project: the U.S. military's efforts to create an atomic bomb during World War II

meteorites: pieces of space rock that pass through Earth's atmosphere

microorganisms: extremely small creatures invisible to the human eye

missionary: someone who works to aid those in need, often by spreading their religious beliefs

NASA: the National Aeronautics and Space Administration, an agency of the U.S. government that oversees space exploration and research

nuclear radiation: powerful and potentially harmful energy emitted by certain types of material

nucleus: the center of an atom

particle: the smallest part of an atom

patent: a legal document that gives someone the right to make, use, or sell an invention and prevents others from copying it

physicist: a scientist who studies matter, energy, and how they interact

prejudice: having an opinion about someone based on how they look, where they come from, or what religion they practice

private practice: a private medical business owned and run by a doctor instead of a larger company

racism: discriminatory or abusive behavior toward members of another race

refugees: people who have been forced to leave their homeland to seek safety elsewhere

relocation centers: prison-like camps where Japanese people in America were moved after they had been taken from their homes during World War II

reserve corps: part of the military in addition to the regular military forces

satellites: artificial bodies placed in orbit around Earth or the moon or another planet to collect information, or for communication

sexism: laws or rules that are prejudiced, or discriminate, usually against women, because of gender

sickle cell anemia: a disease that affects the red blood cells

solar energy: power created by the sun's rays

species: any distinct group of animals or plants with similar characteristics

STEM: an acronym referring to the fields of science, technology, engineering, and mathematics

tenure: the right to keep a job permanently

tuberculosis: a highly contagious and life-threatening lung disease

Vietnam War: a conflict lasting from 1955 to 1975, fought between South Vietnam (aided by the United States) and the communist North Vietnam

Select References

Margaret Chung

"The First American-Born Chinese Woman Doctor." *Unladylike2020: The Changemakers*. American Masters, PBS. May 27, 2020. PBS.org/wnet/americanmasters /first-american-born-chinese-woman-doctor-ysk233 /14464.

Rasmussen, Cecilia. "Chinese American Was 'Mom' to 1,000 Servicemen." *Los Angeles Times*. June 24, 2001. LATimes.com/archives/la-xpm-2001-jun-24-me-14223 -story.html.

Wagner, Ella. "Dr. Margaret 'Mom' Chung." National Park Service U.S. Department of the Interior. Accessed August 30, 2021. NPS.gov/people/dr-margaret-mom -chung.htm.

Kazue Togasaki

Beggs, Marjorie. "Pioneering Japanese-American Doctor Remembers Quake, World War II, Her Neighborhoods." *Hoodline*. August 30, 2015. Hoodline.com/2015/08 /kazue-togasaki-quake-world-war-neighborhoods.

"Dr. Kazue Togasaki." National Park Service U.S. Department of the Interior. Accessed September 30, 2021. NPS.gov/people/dr-kazuetogasaki.htm.

Chien-Shiung Wu

Bodden, Valerie. *Nuclear Physicist Chien-Shiung Wu*. Minneapolis: Lerner Publications, 2017.

Smeltzer, Ronald. 2019. "Chien-Shiung Wu." Atomic Heritage Foundation. 2019. AtomicHeritage.org/profile /chien-shiung-wu.

Yomtov, Nelson, and Suzanne Keilson. 2018. *Chien-Shiung Wu: Nuclear Physicist*. Minneapolis: Essential Library.

Isabella Aiona Abbott

Bense, Danika. 2019. "A Celebration of Women's History and Dr. Isabella Aiona Abbott - Ho'oulu." Ho'oulu. Honolulu UH Maui College. March 14, 2019. Maui.Hawaii.edu/hooulu/2019/03/14/a-celebration-of -womens-history-and-dr-isabella-aiona-abbott/.

HistoricHawaii. "Isabella Aiona Abbott." Hawai'i Women's Suffrage Centennial Commemoration. April 28, 2020. WSCC.historichawaii.org/profile /isabellaaionaabbott.

"Isabella Aiona Abbott: Long Story Short with Leslie Wilcox." 2014. PBS Hawai'i. June 17, 2014. PBSHawaii.org/long-story-short-with-leslie-wilcox -isabella-aiona-abbott.

Roseli Ocampo-Friedmann

Hively, Will. 1997. "Looking for Life in All the Wrong Places." *Discover Magazine*. May 1, 1997. DiscoverMagazine.com/the-sciences/looking-for-life -in-all-the-wrong-places.

Voytek, Mary A., Linda Billings, Aaron L. Gronstal, and NASA Astrobiology Institute. *Astrobiology: The*

Story of Our Search for Life in the Universe. Washington, D.C.: National Aeronautics and Space Administration, 2015. Science.NASA.gov/science-red/s3fs-public/atoms /files/Astrobiology%20Comic%20(Issue%205).pdf.

Jacqueline Whang-Peng

"Jacqueline Whang-Peng-Cancer Research Pioneer: Taiwan's First Female Surgeon." Excorp.com. Accessed September 5, 2021. Excorp.com/pdf_2010 /JacquelineWhang-Peng.pdf.

National Taiwan University. "Profiles of Campus People in the News—Mrs. Jacqueline Hwang Peng, A Model for Women Scientists in Taiwan." 2006. NTUweb.cloud.ntu.edu.tw/oldenglish/spotlight /2009/e091207_1.html.

Angelita Castro-Kelly

News, ABS-CBN. 2015. "Filipina Who Dreamed Big: Space Scientist Angelita Castro-Kelly, 73." ABS-CBN News. June 17, 2015. News.ABS-CBN.com/global -filipino/06/17/15/filipina-who-dreamed-big-space -scientist-angelita-castro-kelly-73.

Province of Ilocos Norte Official. "Great Ilocanos Interview Series- Angelita Castro Kelly (Full Interview)." March 6, 2014. YouTube.com/watch?v=IH-zJwhYtWc.

Yap, Aby. "Angelita Castro-Kelly: NASA's Fearless Filipina Diplomat." *Illustrado Magazine*. September 5, 2012. IllustradoLife.com/angelita-castro-kelly-nasas -fearless-filipina-diplomat.

Joan Block

Block, Joan. "Hepatitis B Foundation Executive Director Joan Block Steps Down, but First Shares Her Love Story." Hepatitis B Foundation. May 17, 2017. HepB.org /blog/hepatitis-b-foundation-executive-director-joan -block-steps-first-shares-love-story.

Jenei, Liz. "Joan Block of the Hepatitis B Foundation Honored by Viral Hepatitis Action Coalition of the Centers for Disease Control Foundation." *Roxborough-Manayunk, PA Patch*, Patch, 6 Aug. 2013, Patch.com /pennsylvania/roxborough/joan-block-of-the-hepatitis-b -foundation-honored-by-viral-hepatitis-action-coalition -of-the-centers-for-disease-control-foundation.

Rubel, Gina. "Celebrating AAPI Heritage Month with Joan Block, Co-Founder of the Hepatitis B Foundation." On Record PR, podcast audio. Furia Rubel Communications, Inc. 2020. Accessed September 4, 2021.

Josephine Jue

Jung, Jaewon. "Chinese Americans Heralded for Helping Apollo 11 Land on the Moon." AsAmNews. July 16, 2019. AsAmNews.com/2019/07/16/chinese-american -heralded-for-helping-apollo-11-land-on-the-moon.

Magnolia State Live. 2019. "Mississippi Moonshot: Josephine Jue, Mississippi Native, NASA Mathematician, First Asian-American Woman at NASA." Magnolia State Live. July 19, 2019. MagnoliaStateLive.com/2019 /07/19/mississippi-moonshot-josephine-jue -mississippi-native-nasa-mathematician-first-asian -american-woman-at-nasa.

Fan Rong King Chung Graham

Butler, Steve. 2020. "The Mathematical Life of Fan Chung." *Notices of the American Mathematical Society* 67 (3): 327–35. AMS.org/journals/notices/202003/rnoti-p327.pdf.

O'Connor, J. J., and E. F. Robertson. "Fan Rong K Chung Graham." MacTutor History of Mathematics Archive. University of St. Andrews. September 2009. MathsHistory.st-andrews.ac.uk/Biographies/Chung.

Weston, Madalyn. "Celebrating Women in STEM: Dr. Fan Chung." *UMKC Roo News.* May 3, 2019. Info.UMKC.edu/unews/celebrating-women-in-stem-dr-fan-chung.

Kalpana Chawla

Mukherjee, Jashodhara. "17 Years after Kalpana Chawla's Death, Her Father Opens Up about Her Dream." News18. October 11, 2020. News18.com/news/buzz/17-years-after-kalpana-chawlas-death-her-father-opens-up-about-her-dream-2941149.html.

Pal, Sanchari. "A Starry-Eyed Girl Called 'Monto': The Untold Story of Kalpana Chawla's Childhood in India." *The Better India.* March 17, 2017. TheBetterIndia.com/91797/kalpana-chawla-karnal-haryana-nasa-columbia.

Tillman, Nola Taylor, and Ailsa Harvey. "Kalpana Chawla: Biography & Columbia Disaster." Space.com, Space, 20 Dec. 2017, Space.com/17056-kalpana-chawla-biography.html.

Alice Min Soo Chun

Gallagher, Tyler. "Meet the Inventors: Alice Min Soo Chun on How to Go from Idea to Store Shelf." *Authority Magazine*. Accessed September 7, 2021. Medium.com /authority-magazine/meet-the-inventors-alice-min -soo-chun-on-how-to-go-from-idea-to-store-shelf -8c5b28e21e54.

"Meet Alice Min Soo Chun, Founder of SEEUS95 Inc, and Solight Design." 2021. Billion Success. January 21, 2021. BillionSuccess.com/alice-min-soo-chun/.

"10 Million Rays of Light | Alice Chun | TEDxBushwick." 2016. TEDx Talks video. June 15, 2016. YouTube.com /watch?v=ko1gkRfX8ys.

Tuyet-Hanh Schnell

Li, Vanessa. 2021. "Lost in Translation: Demystifying and Maximizing Asian Culture - All Together." Alltogether.swe.org. April 14, 2021. AllTogether.swe .org/2021/04/demystifying-asian-culture/.

Society of Women Engineers. "Asian Pacific American Heritage Month: Highlighting Asian American Engineers Pt. 1. All Together (blog). May 4, 2020. AllTogether.swe.org/2020/05/asian-american-pacific -islander-heritage-month-highlighting-asian-american -engineers-pt-1.

Stevens Institute of Technology. "Tuyet-Hanh Schnell '91." Stevens Institute of Technology. March 26, 2021. Stevens.edu/profiles/tuyet-hanh-schnell-91.

Reshma Saujani

Olsen, Chris. "Featured Founder: Reshma Saujani, Girls Who Code." My Founder Story. November 17, 2019. MyFounderStory.com/featured-founder-reshma -saujani-girls-who-code/.

Saujani, Reshma. "Reshma Saujani." Accessed September 8, 2021. ReshmaSaujani.com/about.

———. "Teach Girls Bravery, Not Perfection." Ted video. Accessed September 8, 2021. Ted.com/talks /reshma_saujani_teach_girls_bravery_not_perfection /transcript.

Maryam Mirzakhani

Klarreich, Erica. "A Tenacious Explorer of Abstract Surfaces." *Quanta Magazine.* August 12, 2014. QuantaMagazine.org/maryam-mirzakhani-is-first -woman-fields-medalist-20140812.

Pournader, Mehrdokht (Medo). 2017. "Maryam Mirzakhani Was a Role Model for More than Just Her Mathematics." The Conversation. July 17, 2017. TheConversation.com/maryam-mirzakhani-was-a-role -model-for-more-than-just-her-mathematics-81143.

Rafi, Kasra. "Maryam Mirzakhani (1977–2017)." *Nature* 549, 32 (2017). doi.org/10.1038/549032a.

About the Author

Tina Cho is the author of four picture books: *Rice from Heaven: The Secret Mission to Feed North Koreans* (Little Bee Books 2018), *Korean Celebrations* (Tuttle 2019), *My Breakfast with Jesus: Worshipping God around the World* (Harvest House 2020), and *The Ocean Calls: A Haenyeo Mermaid Story* (Kokila/ Penguin Random House 2020). Her lyrical middle grade graphic novel, *The Other Side of Tomorrow*, debuts from Harper Alley in 2024. After living in South Korea for ten years, Tina, her husband, and two teenagers reside in Iowa, where Tina teaches kindergarten, bringing science and other subjects to life for little kids.

About the Illustrator

María Perera was born in northern Spain. When she was young, she discovered there were few things in life she enjoyed as much as listening to The Beatles and drawing. She graduated with a degree in art history and then studied graphic design. María has worked as a freelance illustrator for international publishers and advertising agencies. She loves to spend time with family and friends.